21st Century Skills **INNOVATION** *Library*

Surgery

by Judy Alter

CHERRY LAKE
Publishing

Published in the United States of America by Cherry Lake Publishing
Ann Arbor, Michigan
www.cherrylakepublishing.com

Content Adviser: Noshene Ranjbar, MD

Design: The Design Lab

Photo Credits: Cover and page 3, ©Rolf Adlercreutz/Alamy; page 4, ©JUPITERIMAGES/
BananaStock/Alamy; page 7, ©Kelpfish, used under license from Shutterstock, Inc.; page 9,
©iStockphoto.com/Acerebel; page 11, ©PHOTOTAKE Inc./Alamy; page 12, ©AP Photo/Charles
Rex Arbogast; page 14, ©ARCTIC IMAGES/Alamy; page 16, ©Sean Nel, used under license from
Shutterstock, Inc.; page 19, ©Rob Byron, used under license from Shutterstock, Inc.; page 21,
©Mark Harmel/Alamy; page 23, ©Classic Image/Alamy; page 25, ©AP Photo/U.S. Marine Corps;
page 27, ©AP Photo/Ed Kolenovsky; page 28, ©AP Photo/Brian Bohannon

Library of Congress Cataloging-in-Publication Data
Alter, Judy, 1938–
Surgery / by Judy Alter.
     p. cm.–(Innovation in medicine)
Includes index.
ISBN-13: 978-1-60279-224-1
ISBN-10: 1-60279-224-0
1. Surgery—History—Juvenile literature. I. Title. II. Series.
RD19.A48 2009
617—dc22   2008006520

Cherry Lake Publishing would like to acknowledge the work of
The Partnership for 21st Century Skills.
Please visit www.21stcenturyskills.org for more information.

CONTENTS

CHAPTER ONE

A Brief History of Surgery

"Well, Harry, the nurse tells me you are going to need some stitches," said Dr. Lopez as he walked into the examining room.

"I've never had stitches before. Is it going to hurt?" asked Harry fearfully.

"Calm down, Harry, it will be fine," said his mom. "I'll be right here, holding your hand."

"Mom! I don't need you to hold my hand!"

Dr. Lopez smiled. "I can guarantee that it will hurt less than falling off of your skateboard and cutting your knee open on the curb. We'll give you a shot to numb the area I'll be stitching. You probably won't feel a thing."

"Really? I'm not going to feel the needle sticking into me as you stitch it up?"

"Nope, you won't," replied Dr. Lopez. "But you're lucky to be living today and not hundreds of years ago.

Surgeons complete years of training and stay current on the latest medical procedures.

Back then surgery was new. You wouldn't believe what surgery used to be like back then."

❋ ❋ ❋

Have you had your tonsils removed? Or has a friend of yours had an appendix removed? These and many other procedures are surgeries. They involve cutting into live **tissue**. Hair, fingernails, and toenails are dead tissue, so cutting them doesn't count.

In some cases, surgery is the repairing of wounds. In those cases, the patient's tissue was already cut and needs to be repaired.

Life & Career Skills

Surgeons (doctors who perform surgery) work with pathologists (physicians who analyze tissue to study the origin and course of a disease) to diagnose health problems. For examples, a surgeon may **biopsy** a mole that has recently grown and changed in appearance. Then the surgeon sends the tissue sample to a pathologist, who studies it under a microscope to determine if it is **benign** or **malignant**. By working together, these doctors are able to choose the appropriate treatment for their patients.

More than 15 million people in the United States have surgery every year. Surgery can repair broken bones, remove diseased parts of the body, prevent chronic or continued pain, or help diagnose a health problem.

Surgery today is far safer and less painful than it was in the past. Modern surgical knowledge is the result of observations and experiments by skilled surgeons over many centuries. They developed ways to better control the three main problems associated with surgery: bleeding, infection, and pain.

The oldest form of surgery is trepanation—drilling or scraping a hole in the skull to relieve pressure on the brain. Archaeologists have found evidence of such surgery as early as 3300 BCE. They have concluded that many such surgical wounds healed and the patients survived.

In early times, surgery no doubt began with a health crisis. The patient either would not survive without surgery or was in unbearable pain. Bleeding that could not be stopped, called hemorrhaging, required immediate action.

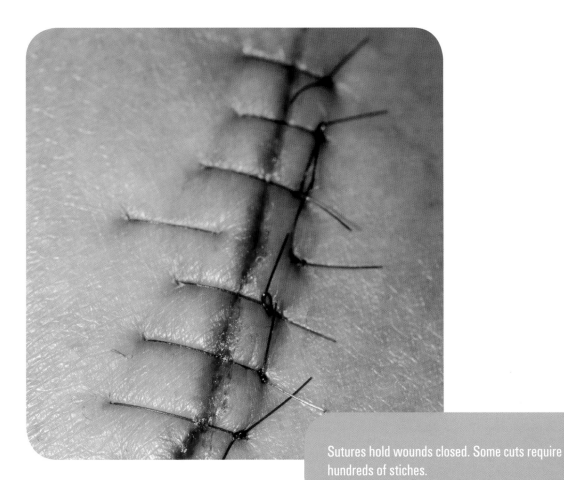

Sutures hold wounds closed. Some cuts require hundreds of stiches.

People used a variety of materials to protect wounds and to control bleeding. Sometimes tar or clay was used. Cobwebs were also commonly used. In cold climates, wounds were packed with snow; in warm climates, hot leaves or hot sand were used. The extreme heat of hot brands (similar to hot irons) was used to seal off bleeding veins and arteries. This is called cauterization. In early times, it was extremely painful and often unsuccessful. **Sutures** have been used to close wounds for thousands of years. Ligatures are bindings (materials that hold something together) made with thread, silk, or linen. They are used to tie a bleeding blood vessel and stop hemorrhaging. They were used as early as the Middle Ages. With all of these methods, there was a large risk of infection.

By the 15th century, surgeons were encouraged to study for many years before practicing surgery. Surgery began to be taught as a distinct subject in universities. By the 19th century, bachelor's degrees in surgery were offered, and then master's degrees.

Methods to control hemorrhaging, pain, and infection brought about the era of modern surgery, which is just more than a century old. In the 20th century, developments in surgery were rapid. Heart surgery became practical, eye surgery was improved, and microsurgery (surgery done under a microscope) was developed. In addition, **cosmetic** surgery became common, transplant surgery became a reality, and the **laser** often replaced the **scalpel** in surgery.

Today, surgeries are often divided into two types: those that are necessary for the patient's health and well-being, and those that the patient elects, or chooses, to have.

CHAPTER TWO

The Development of New Techniques

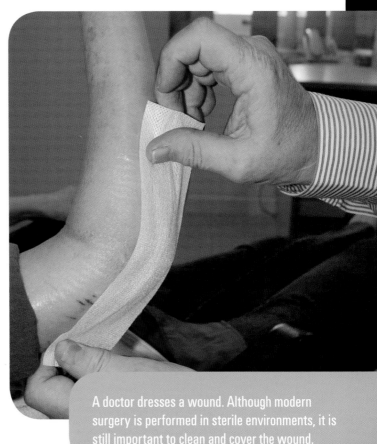

Probably the most important early innovation in surgery was the control of infection. In the early 19th century, most physicians believed that infection was caused by exposing body tissue to oxygen. They thought they could help avoid infection by covering wounds with something. They did not wash their hands after treating patients, even after surgery. Almost half of surgical patients died

A doctor dresses a wound. Although modern surgery is performed in sterile environments, it is still important to clean and cover the wound.

because of post-operative infection. The surgeons didn't realize that their hands were carrying bacteria and other infectious **microbes** from one patient to another.

Dr. Joseph Lister studied infected wounds at the Glasgow Royal Infirmary in Scotland in the 1860s. His studies confirmed Louis Pasteur's idea that infection is caused by microbes. When microbes enter tissue, they cause infection and decay. Lister concluded that the microbes had to be destroyed so they couldn't infect patients' wounds. At the time, carbolic acid was used to **deodorize** rotting garbage. Thinking creatively, Lister used a carbolic acid solution on surgical wounds. Soon after he began using this solution, his patients at the infirmary remained nearly free of infection.

More major innovations came in the early 20th century. Most were the result of physicians observing their patients and thinking about surgical techniques that might do less damage to body tissue. They knew that patients would bleed less if less tissue were damaged. The patients would also have less pain.

Laparoscopic surgery combines a small incision and the use of light as well as a lens or a camera. It was developed in Europe in the early 1900s. Dr. Georg Kelling of Germany performed this type of surgery on dogs. In 1910, Dr. Hans Christian Jacobaeus first used this technique on a human. Since then, several physicians

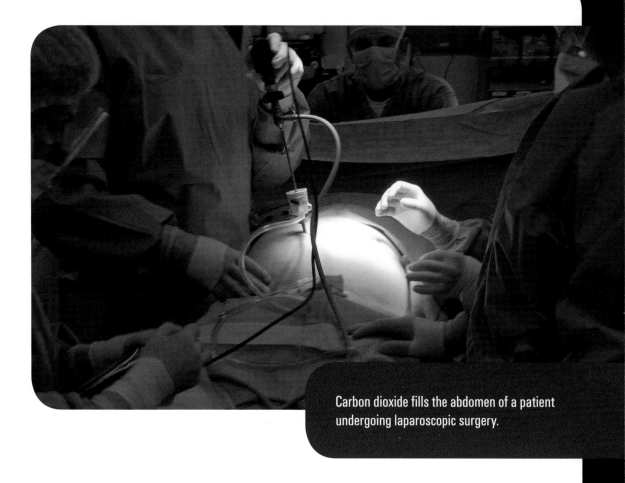

Carbon dioxide fills the abdomen of a patient undergoing laparoscopic surgery.

have experimented with the technique and improved it. In laparoscopic surgery, a small incision is made. Then, carbon dioxide is pumped into the area to move the **abdominal** wall and organs out of the way. Next, a camera is placed in the abdominal cavity. The surgeon can see the organs without looking directly at them. (Sometimes dye is used to help the surgeon better see what he or she is working on.) Laparoscopic surgery is performed for **gallbladder** removal and many other procedures.

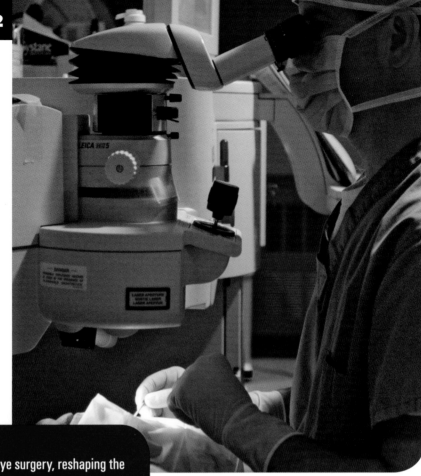

A doctor performs laser eye surgery, reshaping the patient's cornea.

Other scientists discovered that certain types of lasers could be used to cut into human tissue with little damage to surrounding tissues. Laser surgery uses precisely focused light that heats targeted cells until they burst. Surgeons can use a laser to remove tumors of the brain, liver, or other organs. It can seal small blood vessels or reduce swelling. Laser surgery is used to improve vision by reshaping the cornea. Lasers are also used for cosmetic procedures—to remove wrinkles, tattoos, and birthmarks.

Many parts of the human body are very small and delicate. Some creative surgeons figured out that working with the aid of a microscope would make it easier to treat these hard-to-see parts. This type of surgery is called microsurgery. In 1960, Dr. Jules Jacobson at the University of Vermont used a microscope to join very small blood vessels.

American plastic surgeon Dr. Harry J. Buncke was so intrigued by the idea of microsurgery that he experimented with microsurgical techniques in his lab at home. He created very thin nylon sutures and fastened them to handmade needles. These needles could then be used for operating on blood vessels that are 1 millimeter (0.03937 inch) in diameter. That is the size of the major blood vessels supplying skin and muscles in the human body.

Surgeons who perform microsurgery use very small instruments. These instruments are operated while viewing the affected area through a microscope. Traditional instruments were adapted or made smaller to fit the microsurgery technique. Microsurgery is particularly useful in vascular surgery (surgery on blood vessels). This technique allows surgeons to reattach the small blood vessels in hands, arms, feet, and legs that have been cut off. Microsurgery is also used by plastic surgeons and surgeons who operate on the inner ear or vocal cords. It can be used for eye surgery, too.

An operation on any part of the body poses specific challenges. For a long time, operating on the cardiovascular system (the heart and blood vessels) was thought to be too dangerous to even consider. That's because this system is responsible for keeping all the other systems running. It pumps blood to all the body's tissues.

In 1951, Dr. William T. Mustard of Toronto performed the first surgery using a heart-lung bypass machine. This machine revolutionized heart surgery. It provides artificial circulation to a patient while surgeons

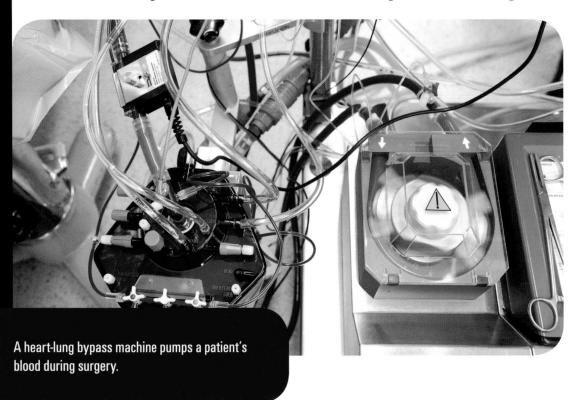

A heart-lung bypass machine pumps a patient's blood during surgery.

work on the heart. Blood that normally would go from the heart to the lungs for oxygen instead is drained from the heart. It is then sent through an artificial lung, where it is exposed to oxygen. After receiving oxygen, the blood is pumped back into the patient's body for circulation. This allows surgeons to stop the heart for several hours while they operate on it.

Surgeons often remove diseased tissue or repair damaged tissue. Some surgeons looked for ways to completely replace damaged tissue. Their work led to organ transplantation. Transplant surgery poses additional problems that must be overcome. A transplanted organ can be rejected by the patient's **immune system**. If the system doesn't recognize the tissue cells of the transplanted organ, it will attack the foreign tissue. In the first successful human-to-human kidney transplant, the donor and the recipient were identical twins. The donated organ wasn't rejected because identical twins' tissues are identical. Because of this, the recipient's immune system didn't attack the donated kidney. This surgery was performed in 1954.

CHAPTER THREE

Using New Techniques

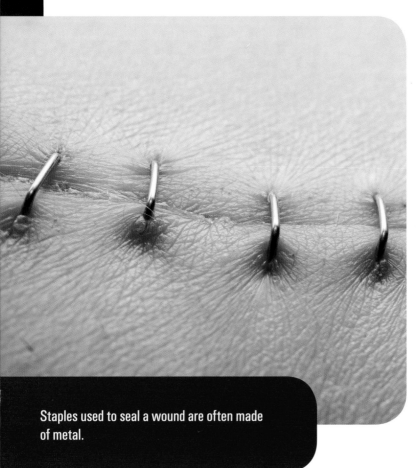

Staples used to seal a wound are often made of metal.

Many innovations come about when procedures are improved upon or applied in new ways. Sutures used today to close surgical wounds don't look like those used thousands of years ago. Back then, wounds were sometimes stitched up using thorns as needles and plant fibers for sutures. Today, some sutures dissolve in the body. The patient doesn't have to be cut open again just to have the stitches removed. Surface or skin stitches are easily and painlessly removed. Today, staples are also used on the skin, as are special kinds of glue.

Successful transplant surgery began in 1954 with the transplant of a kidney. Physicians have been able to apply those techniques to a variety of other organs. In 1967, Dr. Christiaan Barnard, a surgeon in South Africa, performed the first human-to-human heart transplant. He transplanted the heart of a young woman killed in a car accident into the chest of a middle-aged man. The man had to take medication so his body wouldn't reject the heart. This medication weakened his immune system, and he contracted pneumonia. He died 18 days after the transplant.

Since then, researchers have developed tests to help determine better organ matches for transplants. Medications that lessen the likelihood of rejection are now available. New techniques keep organs alive longer outside the body. Today, about 2,000 heart transplants are performed in the United States each year. Many more patients die of heart failure while waiting for a transplant because there are more people that need heart transplants than there are donors.

An artificial heart could solve many of the problems of heart transplant surgery. An artificial heart is a

Learning & Innovation Skills

 One of the most startling uses of transplant surgery has been facial transplants. This surgery has been performed on only a handful of people. Each of the patients had severely disfigured faces as a result of accidents or animal attacks. Surgeons refined methods developed for both microsurgery and transplantation to transplant a face. The technique is so new that improvements are bound to come in the future. Doctors keep experimenting to find ways to improve the procedure and make it less painful for the patient.

mechanical device that takes over the function of the heart. It is sometimes used to prolong a patient's life while he or she awaits a donor heart. But right now, artificial hearts aren't effective for long enough to be used as permanent replacements for failing hearts.

Paul Winchell was the first to develop an artificial heart. He gave the patent for it to the University of Utah in 1963. Dr. Robert Jarvik used Winchell's invention as a model for his own artificial heart, called the Jarvik-7. In 1982, the Jarvik-7 was placed in a patient named Barney Clark. He lived 112 days with his artificial heart.

Doctors continue to work on refining the artificial heart. They are also working on other devices that help a heart that is too weak to pump blood through the body.

Laparoscopic surgery has also been improved upon in the years since it was first invented. Originally intended for abdominal surgeries, it has now been adapted for use in **orthopedic** surgery. Using a laparoscope, surgeons can insert a pin to stabilize a fractured bone without making a large incision.

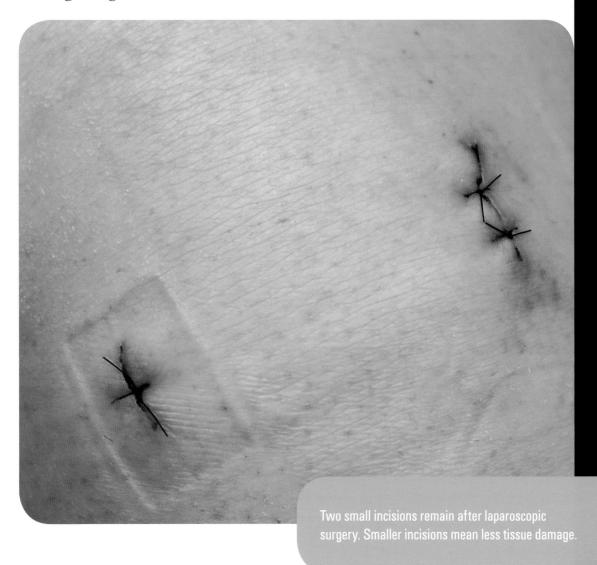

Two small incisions remain after laparoscopic surgery. Smaller incisions mean less tissue damage.

CHAPTER FOUR

The Future of Surgery

The possibilities seem endless for new surgical innovations. Researchers and surgeons around the world are looking for ways to improve upon and apply surgical techniques.

Some researchers are working with high intensity focused ultrasound (HIFU) technology. It uses focused sound waves to destroy diseased tissue. It is even more effective than a laser at killing unwanted tissue without damaging surrounding tissue. It does not require an incision, so it is sometimes referred to as **noninvasive**.

One of the most revolutionary developments on the surgical horizon is robotic surgery. Ideal for small, contained spaces, a surgical robot with tiny instruments is controlled by the surgeon's hands. The result is minimal invasion of the body and a small incision. Surgical robots

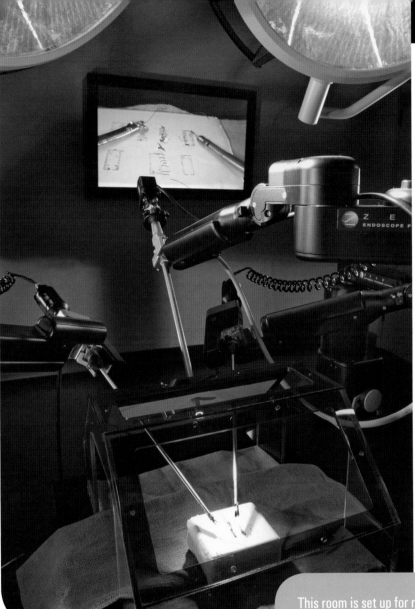

This room is set up for robotic surgery training. Surgeons must practice with new technologies before using them on patients.

have been used in procedures on several parts of the body, including the heart. Researchers continue to look for ways to make the robots even smaller.

Learning & Innovation Skills

 New surgical techniques are often developed to treat one specific disease. Then, doctors observe the technique and realize it has other potential applications. Have you ever learned a new skill in one school subject and then realized you could apply the same skill in a different way in another subject? What was the skill? How did you adapt it?

Advances in surgical techniques have led to changes in other aspects of health care, too. As laparoscopic and other less invasive techniques have become more common, the length of hospital stays has decreased. In fact, many surgeries are now performed as outpatient procedures. This means that the patient doesn't spend the night in the hospital. Instead, he or she goes home a few hours after the surgery has been performed.

As medical schools find ways to attract and train more and better surgeons, new surgical techniques are sure to follow. What lies on the surgical frontier? Only the most creative minds in medicine know the answer.

CHAPTER FIVE

Some Famous Medical Innovators

Many people have made contributions to the field of surgery. Here are just a few of the key innovators.

Joseph Lister

Joseph Lister studied medicine in London. In 1861, he was appointed surgeon at the Glasgow Royal

Treating surgical wounds with carbolic acid solution, Joseph Lister was the first to perform antiseptic surgery.

Infirmary in Scotland. It was there that he developed his theories of **antiseptic** surgery. But many English colleagues doubted Lister's theory. He decided he had to convince London doctors of his theory. In 1877, he was offered the chair of clinical surgery at King's College in London. He demonstrated his technique on the repair of a fractured kneecap, a difficult operation that often resulted in infection and death. The operation was successful, and the London surgeons were convinced.

Dwight Harken

Dr. Dwight Harken was a pioneer of heart surgery. During World War II (1939–1945), doctors in the battlefields pioneered advances in antibiotics, anesthesia, and blood transfusions. Harken used these improved techniques to gain access to the heart, an organ that many doctors thought was too delicate to tamper with. He first operated on animals, trying to develop a technique that would allow him to cut into a still-beating heart to remove **shrapnel**. He operated on three groups of 14 animals. In the first group, all died; in the second, half died; in the third, only 2 died. Then he applied his techniques to human patients. All the patients survived. He proved that the human heart could be operated on. Harken's technique was soon applied to heart valves that no longer worked properly.

Medical workers treat a wounded U.S. soldier on the battlefield during World War II. The methods used by field doctors during the war inspired Dwight Harken to attempt heart surgery.

Learning & Innovation Skills

 Some of the greatest innovations come about when people from different fields work together. Dr. Michael DeBakey collaborated with Dr. George Noon, a fellow surgeon at Baylor College of Medicine, and David Saucier, a NASA engineer and former patient. They developed one of the first ventricular assist devices (VADs), or heart pumps. It is called the DeBakey VAD.

Michael DeBakey

While serving as a surgeon in the military during World War II, Dr. Michael DeBakey proposed the idea of Mobile Army Surgical Hospitals, or MASH units. These units could provide prompt medical treatment to severely wounded soldiers. In 1948, he became chair of the Cora and Webb Mading Department of Surgery at the Baylor University College of Medicine in Houston. There, he performed one of the first coronary-artery bypass surgeries. This procedure is done to improve blood flow to the heart by bypassing a clogged artery in the heart.

In 1953, DeBakey was the first to perform a successful carotid endarterectomy. This is a procedure that removes build-up inside the carotid arteries in the neck and restores blood flow to the brain. In 1965, he was on the cover of *Time* magazine, which honored his pioneering work and innovations in cardiovascular surgery and the artificial heart.

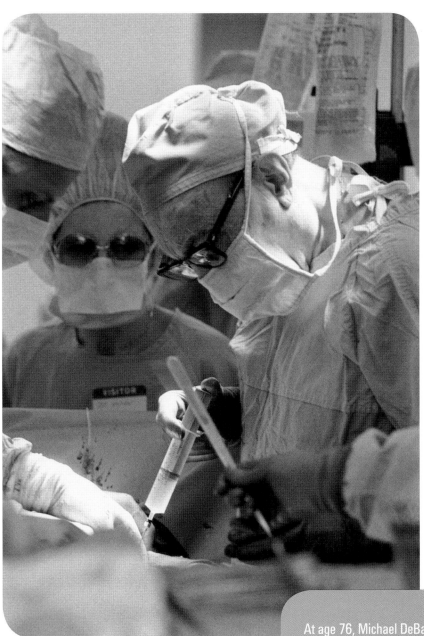

At age 76, Michael DeBakey operates on a patient's heart in 1985.

Harry J. Buncke

In a 1964 medical journal, Dr. Harry J. Buncke reported that he had reattached a rabbit ear that had been cut off. This was the first report of someone successfully working with extremely small blood vessels. Two years

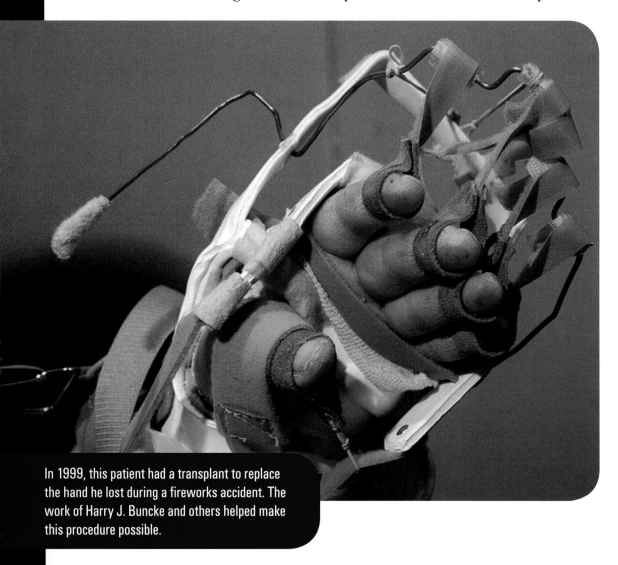

In 1999, this patient had a transplant to replace the hand he lost during a fireworks accident. The work of Harry J. Buncke and others helped make this procedure possible.

later, he and colleagues transplanted a monkey's great toe to the animal's hand. After that, reattachment, or replantation, of amputated fingers, toes, legs, and arms was considered possible.

The first successful transplant that required working with extremely small blood vessels in a human patient was in 1969. Buncke transplanted a piece of tissue from a patient's abdomen onto that patient's scalp. Before his death in May 2008, Buncke was director of the Buncke Clinic, an institute for plastic and reconstructive surgery in San Francisco, California. Surgeons at this clinic have accomplished many firsts—human toe-to-hand transplants, scalp replantations, and the replantation of a severed tongue.

Glossary

abdominal (ab-DOM-in-uhl) having to do with the abdomen, the part of the body between the chest and the hips

antiseptic (an-ti-SEP-tik) preventing the growth of germs

benign (bih-NINE) harmless

biopsy (BYE-ahp-see) to remove and examine a small sample of tissue from a living body

cosmetic (kahz-MEH-tik) done for the sake of changing the way a person looks

deodorize (dee-OH-duh-rize) to remove an unpleasant odor

gallbladder (GAWL-bla-duhr) an organ that holds a fluid used to digest food

immune system (ih-MYOON SISS-tuhm) the mechanism by which the body protects itself from disease

laser (LAY-zur) an instrument that creates a powerful beam of light

malignant (muh-LIG-nuhnt) containing cancerous cells

microbes (MY-krobz) very small organisms

noninvasive (non-in-VAY-siv) concerning a medical procedure that doesn't involve an incision into a living body

orthopedic (or-thuh-PEE-dik) relating to the field of medicine that deals with bones and joints

scalpel (SKAL-puhl) a small, straight knife used in surgery

shrapnel (SHRAP-nuhl) bits of metal from an exploding shell or bomb

sutures (SOO-churz) fibers used to sew parts of a living body; stitches made with such fibers

tissue (TIH-shyoo) a mass of cells that forms a particular part of a plant or animal

For More Information

BOOKS

Bankston, John. *Joseph Lister and the Story of Antiseptics*. Hockessin, DE: Mitchell Lane Publishers, 2005.

Fullick, Ann. *Frontiers of Surgery*. Chicago: Heineman Library, 2006.

Townsend, John. *Scalpels, Stitches and Scars: A History of Surgery*. Chicago: Raintree, 2006.

WEB SITES

Bureau of Labor Statistics: Doctor
www.bls.gov/k12/help06.htm
Find out more about what it takes to become a surgeon

KidsHealth for Kids: What Happens in the Operating Room?
www.kidshealth.org/kid/feel_better/places/or.html
For information about what happens during surgery

Index

About the Author

Judy Alter grew up in a family that included 18 physicians and spent many of her younger years working in hospitals and medical schools. The director of Texas Christian University Press, she is the author of numerous books for both children and adults. She is the mother of four and grandmother of seven. Ms. Alter lives in Fort Worth, Texas, with her dog and cat.